D0097642

The Wit and Wisdom
of Robert E. Lee

Photo of Gen. Robert E. Lee by Mathew Brady, 1865.

The Wit and Wisdom of Robert E. Lee

Edited by Devereaux D. Cannon, Jr.

PELICAN PUBLISHING COMPANY
Gretna 2004

First printing, November 1997
Second printing, October 1998
Third printing, August 2000
Fourth printing, August 2004

*The word "Pelican" and the depiction of a pelican are trademarks
of Pelican Publishing Company, Inc., and are registered
in the U.S. Patent and Trademark Office.*

Library of Congress Cataloging-in-Publication Data

Lee, Robert E. (Robert Edward), 1807-1870.
    The wit and wisdom of Robert E. Lee / edited by Devereaux D. Cannon.
      p. cm.
    ISBN 1-56554-275-4
    1. Lee, Robert E. (Robert Edward), 1807-1870—Quotations.
    2. Quotations, American. I. Cannon Devereaux D., 1954- II. Title.
E467.1.L4A25 1997
973.7'092—dc21
                                      97-23683
                                        CIP

Manufactured in the United States of America
Published by Pelican Publishing Company, Inc.
1000 Burmaster Street, Gretna, Louisiana 70053

*This little book is dedicated
to Nancy Katherine ("Kate") Cannon,
her father's "precious life."*

Contents

Introduction

On May 31, 1862, the Southern Confederacy appeared ready for her national grave. Her enemies were pressing her on all sides. Kentucky was lost, along with most of Tennessee and Missouri. New Orleans had fallen, and Northern forces occupied the barrier islands of Georgia and the Carolinas. U.S. Gen. George McClellan's 100,000-man army had pushed up the Virginia peninsula to the very suburbs of Richmond; and the Confederate army's commander, Gen. Joseph E. Johnston, was cut down with serious wounds. With his nation facing extinction, President Davis turned over the army to the only general of rank on the scene, Robert Edward Lee.

Lee entered Confederate service as a bright star. He had turned down an offer to command the United States forces in favor of the offer to command Virginia's army. After Virginia's forces were consolidated with those of the Confederate States, Lee became military adviser to President Davis. When Lee was given command of the army outside of Richmond, a concerned member of Johnston's staff asked Joseph Ives of the president's staff if Lee could save the country from disaster. Ives responded that if it could be done, Lee could do it, for Lee was "audacity personified. His name is audacity."

Lee did seem like a warrior-saint sent to save his country in its time of need. Against all hope, he freed Richmond from the threat of McClellan's army and sent it reeling back down the peninsula. With the audacity predicted by Ives, he went on the offensive, defeating the enemy at the second battle of Manassas;

but he had his offensive blunted at Sharpsburg. Again turning defeat into victory, he prevailed at Fredericksburg and Chancellorsville. Always giving credit to God for his successes, he placed blame for his loss at Gettysburg on his own shoulders. In the final grinding year and a half of war, Lee won victories at places such as the Wilderness and Spotsylvania—victories only Lee could have won. Although his country was not destined to prevail in its struggle for independence, his native brilliance, combined with his selfless service to his people, assured immortality to Robert E. Lee.

In many ways the immortality has served to obscure the real Robert Lee. The Lee imagined in legend has been described as the Marble Man. The Robert E. Lee who lived was a very real human being: a warm and loving husband and father; a devoted Christian well aware of his own shortfalls; and a soldier who *thought* about life, loved beauty, and was pained by the destruction to nature and humanity that his profession caused.

Lee was most open and intimate with his own family. Most of the quotes in this book are drawn from letters to his wife and children. Lee married Mary Anne Custis, daughter and heiress of George Washington's adopted son, George Washington Parke Custis, in 1831. Robert and Mary Lee had seven children. In 1861 all of the sons were of military age—Custis, 29; Fitzhugh (Rooney), 24; and Robert, Jr. (Rob), 18. All served in the Confederate States army. Custis served on President Davis's staff and in the Corps of Engineers, Rooney became a cavalry commander, and Rob served as a private in the artillery. The daughters were Mary (age 26 in 1861), Annie (who died at age 22 in 1862), Agnes (age 20 in 1861), and Mildred (who was 15 in 1861 and who was called "Precious Life" by her father).

The quotations in this book were written mostly in a nine-teenth-century informal style. That style used a large number of abbreviations. For the most part, those abbreviations have been left as Lee wrote them. The one significant editorial change was to replace the ampersand [&], which he used throughout his letters, with the full word *and* so that the modern reader might not be distracted.

What follows is not a complete collection of Lee's thoughts and words, but rather a few selected quotations that I hope will give the reader an insight into the man called General Lee, and perhaps some inspiration.

The Wit and Wisdom
of Robert E. Lee

Lee on Life

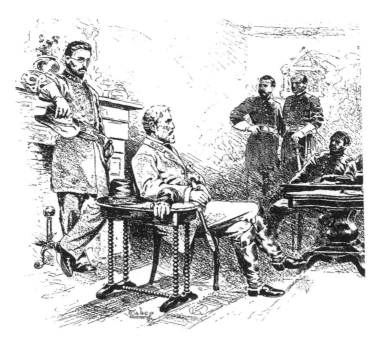

Too much application to mathematical problems at night, with the unknown quantities X and Y represented by a demijohn and tumbler, was very apt to have for a result a head ache next morning.[1]

Dissimilar as are characters, intellects, and situations, the great duty of life is the same, the promotion of the happiness and welfare of our fellow men.[2]

---

1. Lee to his aide, Lt. Col. Charles Marshall, who was suffering with a headache one morning in the fall of 1862.
2. Undated notes in Lee's diary.

Cleanliness, temperance and order [are] very promotive of health and cheerfulness.[3]

[Turn] your affliction to your benefit.[4]

---

3. Letter to Custis Lee, 13 April 1851.
4. Lee to Agnes Lee, 11 August 1855.

The march of Providence is so slow and our desires so impatient; the work of progress is so immense and our means of aiding it so feeble; the life of humanity is so long, that of the individual so brief, that we often see only the ebb of the advancing wave and are thus discouraged. It is history that teaches us to hope.[5]

I am opposed to the theory of doing wrong that good may come of it. I hold to the belief that you must act right whatever the consequences.[6]

---

5. R. E. Lee Headquarters Papers, Virginia Historical Society, Richmond.
6. Letter to Custis Lee, 22 June 1851.

am fond of independence. It is that feeling that prompts me to come up strictly to the requirements of law and regulations. I wish neither to seek or receive indulgence from anyone.[7]

Shake off those gloomy feelings. Drive them away. Fix your mind and pleasures upon what is before you. . . . All is bright if you will think it so. All is happy if you will make it so.[8]

When a thing is *done* we ought always make the best of it.[9]

---

7. Letter to Custis Lee, 22 June 1851.
8. Letter to Custis Lee, 28 March 1852.
9. Letter to Custis Lee, 28 March 1852.

What a glorious world Almighty God has given us. How thankless and ungrateful we are, and how we labour to mar His gifts. May He have mercy on us![10]

Do not *dream*. It is too ideal, too imaginary. . . . Live in the world you inhabit. Look upon things as they are. Take them as you find them. Make the best of them. Turn them to your advantage.[11]

Duty is the sublimest word in our language.[12]

---

10. Letter to his wife, 4 August 1861.
11. Letter to Custis Lee, 28 March 1852.
12. Quote in a letter supposedly from Lee to Custis Lee, dated 5 April 1852, first published in the New York *Sun* 26 November 1864 and exposed by Lee as a forgery when it was reprinted in a Richmond newspaper a short time later.

Young men must not expect to escape contact with evil, but must learn not to be contaminated by it. That virtue is worth but little that requires constant watching and removal from temptation.[13]

It is not necessary for young ladies to become etherial to grow wise.[14]

[The exercise of self-denial and self-control] is the true means of establishing a virtuous character, so far as it can be accomplished by human means.[15]

---

13. Lee to Martha Custis Williams, 16 September 1853.
14. Letter to Annie Lee, 2 March 1862.
15. Letter to his wife, 31 January 1857.

The doctrines and miracles of our Savior have required nearly two thousand years to convert but a small part of the human race, and even among Christian nations what gross errors still exist![16]

I have a beautiful white beard. It is much admired. At least, much remarked on. You know I have told you not to believe what the young men may tell you.[17]

---

16. Letter to his wife, 27 December 1856.
17. Letter to Mildred Lee, 15 November 1861.

In this time of great suffering to the state and country, our private distresses we must bear with resignation like Christians and not aggrevate [*sic*] them by repining, trusting to a kind and merciful God to overrule them for our good.[18]

Everybody is slandered, even the good. How should I escape?[19]

---

18. Letter to his wife, 11 June 1861.
19. Letter to his wife, 9 September 1861.

In times like these, the advancement of some praiseworthy object should be our only aim. The practice of self denial and self sacrifice even was never more urgently demanded.[20]

We cannot always be successful and reverses must come. May God give us courage, endurance, and faith to strive to the end.[21]

20. Letter to his wife, 24 June 1861.
21. Letter to Custis Lee, 3 September 1861.

cannot see what you are proud of and advise you against all such feelings for you know what is said in the good book about a proud spirit going before a fall.[22]

Gain knowledge and virtue and learn your duty to God and your neighbour. That is the great object of life.[23]

You must endeavour to enjoy the pleasure of doing good. That is all that makes life valuable.[24]

---

22. Letter to Mildred Lee, 28 July 1862.
23. Letter to Mildred Lee, 25 December 1862.
24. Letter to his wife, 29 January 1863.

You have only to do what is right. It will become easier by practice, and you will always enjoy in the midst of your trials, the pleasure of an approving conscience. That will be worth everything else.[25]

The more you know, the more you find there is to know in this grand and beautiful world. It is only the ignorant who suppose themselves omniscient.[26]

25. Letter to Mildred Lee, 10 September 1863.
26. Letter to Mildred Lee, 10 September 1863.

We have only to do our whole duty, and everything will be well.[27]

Cupid is always busy when Mars is quiet and our young heroes think it necessary to be killed in some way.[28]

Do not leave Virginia. Our country needs her young men now.[29]

---

27. Letter to Pres. Jefferson Davis, 14 June 1864.
28. Letter to Agnes Lee, 20 November 1864.
29. Lee to a young veteran after the surrender.

True patriotism sometimes requires of men to act exactly contrary, at one period, to that which it does at another, and the motive which impels them—the desire to do right—is precisely the same. The circumstances which govern their actions change; and their conduct must conform to the new order of things.[30]

We have but one rule here, and it is that every student must be a gentleman.[31]

---

30. Letter to Gen. P. G. T. Beauregard, 3 October 1865.
31. Lee to a new student at Washington College.

Education embraces the physical, moral and intellectual instruction of a child from infancy to manhood. Any system is imperfect which does not combine them all.[32]

A dead letter inspires disrespect for the whole body of laws.[33]

As a general principal you should not *force* young men to do their duty, but let them do it voluntarily and thereby develop their characters.[34]

---

32. Letter to J. B. Minor, 17 January 1867.
33. Lee to a group of professors during his presidency at Washington College.
34. Lee during his presidency at Washington College.

You cannot be a true man until you learn to obey.[35]

The gentleman does not needlessly or unnecessarily remind an offender of a wrong he may have committed against him. He can not only forgive, he can forget; and he strives for that nobleness of self and mildness of character which imparts sufficient strength to let the past be the past.[36]

---

35. Lee to students at Washington College.
36. Statement found among Lee's papers after his death.

Study hard, be always a gentleman, live cleanly and remember God, and be peaceable.[37]

However long you live and whatever you accomplish, you will find that the time you spent in the Confederate army was the most profitably spent portion of your life.[38]

Strike the tent.[39]

---

37. Lee to students at Washington College.
38. Lee to Milton W. Humphreys, 1867.
39. Lee's last words, 12 October 1870.

Lee on Family and Children

I wish boys would do what is right; it would be so much easier for all parties![1]

You do not know how much I have missed you and the children, my dear Mary. To be alone in a crowd is very solitary.[2]

When love influences the parent the child will be activated by the same spirit.[3]

---

1. Lee to Robert E. Lee, Jr., about 1853.
2. Letter to his wife, 5 June 1839.
3. Undated notes in Lee's diary.

ou . . . will have to exercise firm authority over all of [the children]. This will not require severity, or even strictness but constant attention and an unwavering course. Mildness and forbearance, tempered by firmness and judgment, will strengthen their affection for you, while it will maintain your control over them.[4]

We must not for our own pleasure lose sight of the interest of our children.[5]

---

4. Letter to his wife, 5 June 1839.
5. Letter to his wife, 2 January 1851.

expect to die a pauper, and I see no way of preventing it. So that I can get enough for you and the girls I am content.[6]

Cut off from all communication with you and my children, my greatest pleasure is to write to you and them.[7]

You know what confidence I have in the powers of my children. You would have soon made me well, for you could have taken all my pills, &c. [etc.], and kept the doctors off me.[8]

6. Letter to his wife, 21 December 1862.
7. Letter to his wife, 25 December 1862.
8. Letter to Agnes Lee, 11 April 1863.

Give much love to my "precious life." I am very sorry I could not see her, and God only knows when we shall meet again. She must write to her papa, and not eat plum cakes.[9]

I sincerely join in your wish that the war was over and that we could all be once more united, though it may be for a short time.[10]

---

9. Letter to his wife, 23 May 1863.
10. Letter to Agnes Lee, 25 May 1863.

ou girls have no time to be sick. You have a sacred charge, the care of your poor mother.[11]

Tell Mildred that I felt quite flattered at Custis' visit, but I learned about 10 o'clock last night that Miss Jenny Fairfax and a bevy of young damsels came down in the same train, to attend some festival at an artillery camp. That is the way children humbug their fathers.[12]

11. Letter to Agnes Lee, 25 May 1863.
12. Letter to his wife, 17 January 1865.

Neither violence nor harshness should ever be used [in child rearing], and the parent must bear constantly in mind, that to govern his child, he must show him that he can control himself.[13]

But though age with its snow has whitened my head, and its frost has stiffened my limbs, my heart, you well know, is not frozen to you, and summer returns when I see you.[14]

---

13. Letter to J. B. Minor, 17 January 1867.
14. Letter to his wife, 22 June 1862.

Lee on Women

ou are right in my interest in pretty women, and it is strange I do not lose it with age. But I perceive no diminution.[1]

The *wimming*[2] alone show the only true heroism that is here exhibited. To see with what cheerfulness and even pleasure they leave everything behind and enter these forests. . . . They are always ready to offer kindness and relief, are frugal and attentive while their rough consorts are careless[,] unthrifty[,] speculating[,] *lazing[,]* or worse.[3]

---

1. Letter to Henry Kayser, 16 June 1845.
2. Lee writes "wimming" in imitation of the local pronunciation of the word "women" on the Missouri frontier.
3. Letter to Carter Lee, 8 October 1837.

As for the Daughters of Eve in this country [Fort Monroe, Virginia], they are formed in the very poetry of nature, and would make your lips water and fingers tingle.[4]

I have only seen the ladies in this vicinity when flying from the enemy, and it caused me acute grief to witness their exposure and suffering. But a more noble spirit was never displayed anywhere.[5]

---

4. Letter to Jack Mackay, 26 June 1834.
5. Letter to Agnes Lee, 26 December 1862.

ell Mrs. Randolph I have taken some of the blackberry [wine] today and find it very nice. I think though the sight of her would be more beneficial to me.[6]

Miss Jennie Pegram is at present agitating the thoughts of [the young] soldiers in [Petersburg]. I see her bright face occasionally as she flashes it for her beaux, but in pity she turns it away from me, for it is almost dazzling.[7]

---

6. Letter to his wife, 7 June 1864.
7. Letter to Agnes Lee, 20 November 1864.

am glad to hear of Miss Carrie Mason again. I feared the Philistines had her. It is singular however that she and Col[.] Jenifer should visit Richmond at the same time. I fear it is ominous. . . . She must devote herself to her country. If she wants to do a good thing, let her come and see me.[8]

My boys need to be heartened up when they get their furloughs. Go on, look your prettiest, and be just as nice to them as ever you can be![9]

---

8. Letter to his wife, 16 November 1864.
9. Advice to young ladies of Richmond in the Spring of 1864 who were inquiring about whether parties and dances were appropriate in such times.

Lee on Politics

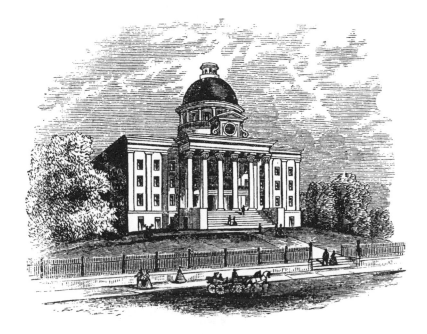

If the Union is dissolved, I shall return to Virginia and share the fortune of my people.[1]

The South has had to bear some hard kicks from all sides.[2]

---

1. Letter to Annette Carter, 16 January 1861.
2. Letter to Andrew Talcott commenting on the Nullification Crisis, 21 February 1833.

There ought to be no "native party" in this country. All ought to be Americans in feelings and acts and more than that none can be.[3]

[It will be seen that the Abolitionists] contend for the ruin of the present American Church and the destruction of the present Union. That the pulpit is denounced as the great stronghold of slavery. The founders of the Constitution and the fathers of the Revolution *Swindlers,* in accomplishing that which after fifty years trial is found to be a curse and not a blessing.[4]

3. Letter to Henry Kayser, 19 December 1845.
4. Letter to Mary Custis, 13 April [year not given, but probably in the 1840s].

In this enlightened age, there are few I believe, but what will acknowledge that slavery as an institution, is a moral and political evil in any Country.[5]

As an American citizen I prize the Union very highly and know of no personal sacrifice that I would not make to preserve it, save that of honour.[6]

---

5. Letter to his wife, 27 December 1856.
6. Letter to Rooney Lee, 3 December 1860.

know no other Country, no other Government, than the *United States* and their *Constitution*.[7]

It has been evident for years that the country was doomed to run the full length of democracy. To what a fearful pass it has brought us. I fear mankind for years will not be sufficiently christianized to bear the absence of restraint and force.[8]

7. Letter to Edward Childe, 9 January 1857.
8. Letter to his wife, 23 January 1861.

Trusting in Almighty God, an approving conscience, and the aid of my fellow-citizens, I devote myself to the service of my native State, in whose behalf alone will I ever again draw my sword.[9]

What has our Congress done to meet the exigency? I may say extremity, in which we are placed?[10]

---

9. Address to the Virginia Convention accepting command of the military and naval forces of the Commonwealth, 22 April 1861.
10. Letter to the Confederate States' Secretary of War James A. Seddon, 10 January 1863.

f honour and independence is delt us I will be content.[11]

The Confederate States have now but one great object in view. The successful issue of their war of independence.[12]

---

11. Letter to Custis Lee, 19 January 1861.
12. Letter to Judge Andrew Magrath, 24 December 1861.

We must make up our minds to fight our battles and win our independence alone. No one will help us.[13]

As far as I have been able to judge, this war presents to the European world but two aspects. A contest in which one party is contending for abstract slavery and the other against it. The existence of vital rights involved does not seem to be understood or appreciated. As long as this lasts, we can expect neither sympathy or aid.[14]

---

13. Letter to his wife, 25 December 1861.
14. Letter to Pres. Jefferson Davis, 6 July 1864.

have great consideration for my African fellow citizens.[15]

It seems to me that we must choose between employing negroes [as soldiers] ourselves, and having them employed against us.[16]

The South has contended only for the supremacy of the constitution, and the just administration of the laws made in pursuance of it.[17]

---

15. Letter to his wife, 18 September 1864.
16. Letter to Pres. Jefferson Davis, 2 September 1864.
17. Letter to Lord Acton, 15 December 1866.

think it the duty of every citizen in the present condition of the country to do all in his power to aid in the restoration of peace and harmony, and in no way to oppose the policy of the State or general government directed to that object.[18]

To the minds of Southern men the idea of "Union" was ridiculous when the States that made the Union did not desire it to continue; but the North fought for the Union, and now, if what appears to be the most powerful party among them is to have its own way, they are doing their best to destroy all real union.[19]

---

18. Letter to the Trustees of Washington College, 24 August 1865.
19. Lee to the Marquess of Lorne, May 1866.

The consolidation of the states into one vast republic, sure to be aggressive abroad and despotic at home, will be the certain precursor of that ruin which has overwhelmed all those that have preceded it.[20]

I grieve for posterity, for American principles and American liberty.[21]

20. Letter to Lord Acton, 15 December 1866.
21. Letter to Annette Carter, 28 March 1868.

Lee on Yankees

Is it not strange that the descendants of those Pilgrim fathers who crossed the Atlantic to preserve their own freedom of opinion, have always proved themselves intolerant of the Spiritual liberty of others?[1]

No civilized nation within knowledge has ever carried on a war as the United States government has against us.[2]

I pray that on this day when "peace and good will" are preached to all mankind, that better thoughts will fill the hearts of our enemies and turn them to peace.[3]

---

1. Letter to his wife, 27 December 1856.
2. Letter to Custis Lee, 19 January 1862.
3. Letter to his wife, 25 December 1862.

am . . . happy in the knowledge that Genl[.] Burnside and his army will not eat their promised Xmas dinner in Richmond to day. I trust they never will.[4]

The yankees have a very coaxing and insidious manner.[5]

Their conduct is not dictated by kindness or love, and therefore we should not expect them to behave otherwise than they do. But I do not think we should follow their example.[6]

---

4. Letter to Mildred Lee, 25 December 1862.
5. Letter to his wife, 8 February 1863.
6. Letter to his wife, 12 July 1863.

Had I foreseen these results of subjugation, I would have preferred to die at Appomattox with my brave men, my sword in this right hand.[7]

---

7. Lee to former Texas governor Fletcher S. Stockdale, August 1870.

Lee on War

The general remedy for the want of success in a military commander is his removal.[1]

The shells thrown from our battery were constant and regular discharges, so beautiful in their flight and so destructive in their fall. It was awful! My heart bled for the inhabitants. The soldiers I did not care so much for, but it was terrible to think of the women and children.[2]

---

1. Letter to Pres. Jefferson Davis, 8 August 1863.
2. Letter to his family, March 1847.

No one at their comfortable homes, can realize the exertions, pains and hardships of an Army in the field, under a scorching sun and in an enervating atmosphere.[3]

It is so much more easy to make heroes on paper than in the field. For one of the latter you meet with 20 of the former, but not until the fight is done.[4]

There is nothing so military as labour and nothing so important to an army as to save the lives of its soldiers.[5]

---

3. Letter to his wife, 12 April 1847.
4. Letter to Jack Mackay, 2 October 1848.
5. Letter to Custis Lee, 23 January 1861.

plan and work with all my might to bring the troops to the right place at the right time; with that I have done my duty. As soon as I order the troops forward into battle, I lay the fate of my army in the hands of God.[6]

It would be a bad thing if I could not rely on my brigade and division commanders.[7]

It is well that war is so terrible; we should grow too fond of it.[8]

---

6. As stated to Capt. Justus Scheibert of the Prussian Army in 1863.
7. As stated to Capt. Justus Scheibert of the Prussian Army in 1863.
8. Lee at Marye's Heights during the battle of Fredericksburg, 13 December 1862.

It is glorious to see such courage in one so young.[9]

It is as impossible for him to have a large operating army at every assailable point in our territory as it is for us to keep one to defend it. We must move our troops from point to point as required, and by close observation and accurate information the true point of attack can generally be ascertained.[10]

---

9. Comment on John Pelham during an artillery duel at the battle of Fredericksburg, 13 December 1862.
10. Letter to Gustavus W. Smith, 4 January 1863.

Everything within the seat of war must be uncertain.[11]

Partial encroachments by the enemy we must expect, but they can always be recovered, and any defeat of their large army will reinstate everything.[12]

I have laid off work enough to employ our people a month. I hope the enemy will be polite enough to wait for us.[13]

---

11. Letter to his wife, 9 September 1861.
12. Letter to Gustavus W. Smith, 4 January 1863.
13. Letter to Annie and Agnes Lee, 22 November 1861.

he best troops are ineffective without good officers.[14]

Nothing can arrest during the present [Lincoln] administration the most desolating war that was ever practiced, except a revolution among their people. Nothing can produce a revolution except systematic success on our part.[15]

[Martial law] should only be resorted to as a last extremity.[16]

---

14. Letter to Judge Andrew Magrath, 24 December 1861.
15. Letter to the Confederate States' Secretary of War James A. Seddon, 10 January 1863.
16. Letter to William Elliot, Edmund Rhett, and Leroy Youmans, 3 December 1861.

f we can baffle them in their various designs this year and our people are true to our cause and not so devoted to themselves and their own aggrandisement, I think our success will be certain.[17]

What a cruel thing war is. To separate and destroy families and friends and mar the purest joys and happiness God has granted us in this world. To fill our hearts with hatred instead of love for our neighbors and to devastate the fair face of this beautiful world.[18]

---

17. Letter to his wife, 19 April 1863.
18. Letter to his wife, 25 December 1862.

One of the miseries of war is that there is no Sabbath and the current of work and strife has no cessation.[19]

I am sorry, as you say, that the movements of the armies cannot keep pace with the expectations of the editors of papers. I know they can regulate matters satisfactorily to themselves on paper. I wish they could do so in the field.[20]

My heart bleeds at the death of every one of our gallant men.[21]

---

19. Letter to Annie Lee, 8 December 1861.
20. Letter to his wife, 7 October 1861.
21. Letter to his wife, 25 December 1862.

We have not remembered that the defenders of a just cause should be pure in [God's] eyes; that our times are in His hands, and we have relied too much on our own arms for the achievement of our independence.[22]

The colonel of a regiment has an important trust, and is a guardian of the State as well as of the lives of her citizens.[23]

---

22. Address to the Army of Northern Virginia, 21 August 1863.
23. Letter to Judge Andrew Magrath, 24 December 1861.

$\mathcal{B}$eyond such assistance as I can give to an invalid wife and three houseless daughters I have no object in life but to devote myself to the defense of our violated country's rights.[24]

Soldiers you know are born to suffer and they cannot escape it.[25]

I am not in favor of retaliation except in very extreme cases, and I think it would be better for us to suffer, and be right in our own eyes and in the eyes of the world.[26]

---

24. Letter to Pres. Jefferson Davis, 22 August 1863.
25. Letter to his wife, 5 April 1863.
26. Letter to Pres. Jefferson Davis, 25 June 1863.

agree with you in believing that our army would be invincible if it could be properly organized and officered. There never were such men in an army before. They will go anywhere and do anything if properly lead.[27]

Today the [railroad] cars have arrived and has brought [*sic*] me a young french officer, full of vivacity and no english, ardent for service with me. I think the appearance of things will cool him[;] if they do not, the night will, for he brought no blankets.[28]

---

27. Letter to Gen. John B. Hood, 21 May 1863.
28. Letter to his wife, 23 February 1863.

e has lost his left arm; but I have lost my right arm.[29]

[Grant's] talent and strategy consists in accumulating overwhelming numbers.[30]

These men are not an army, they are citizens defending their country.[31]

---

29. Lee, 4 May 1863, upon learning that Stonewall Jackson's arm had been amputated.
30. Letter to Custis Lee, 14 July 1864.
31. Lee to A. P. Hill, May 1864.

The lives of our soldiers are too precious to be sacrificed in the attainment of successes that inflict no loss upon the enemy beyond the actual loss in battle.[32]

The soldiers know their duties better than the general officers do.[33]

32. Letter to the Confederate States' Secretary of War James A. Seddon, 10 January 1863.
33. Lee to A. P. Hill, May 1864.

A partisan war may be continued, and hostilities protracted, causing individual suffering and the devastation of the country, but I see no prospect by that means of achieving a separate independence.[34]

The judgment of reason has been displaced by the arbitrament of war.[35]

I know of no fitter resting-place for a soldier than the field on which he has nobly laid down his life.[36]

---

34. Letter to Pres. Jefferson Davis, 20 April 1865.
35. Letter to Lord Acton, 15 December 1866.
36. Lee in 1866 regarding a proposal to remove the remains of the Confederate dead from Gettysburg.

fear we are destined to kill and slaughter each other for ages to come. . . . Whatever may be the issue, I cannot help sympathizing with the struggles of a warlike people to drive invaders from their lands.[37]

After four years of arduous service, marked by unsurpassed courage and fortitude, the Army of Northern Virginia has been compelled to yield to overwhelming numbers and resources.

I need not tell the brave survivors of so many hard fought battles, who have remained steadfast to the last, that I have consented to the result from no distrust of them.

---

37. Observations of Lee on the Franco-Prussian War in a letter of 23 August 1870.

But feeling that valor and devotion could accomplish nothing that would compensate for the loss that must have attended the continuance of the contest, I determined to avoid the useless sacrifice of those whose past services have endeared them to their countrymen.

By the terms of the agreement officers and men can return to their homes and remain until exchanged. You will take with you the satisfaction that proceeds from the consciousness of duty faithfully performed, and I earnestly pray that a Merciful God will extend to you His blessing and protection.

With an increasing admiration of your constancy and devotion to your country, and a grateful remembrance of your kind and generous considerations for myself, I bid you an affectionate farewell.[38]

38. General Order No. 9, 10 April 1865.